How Does It Work?

HOUSEHOLD TECHNOLOGY

**Linda Bruce and
Ian Bruce**

Smart Apple Media

This edition first published in 2006 in the United States of America by Smart Apple Media.

Smart Apple Media
2140 Howard Drive West
North Mankato
Minnesota 56003

First published in 2005 by
MACMILLAN EDUCATION AUSTRALIA PTY LTD
627 Chapel Street, South Yarra, Australia 3141

Visit our Web site at www.macmillan.com.au

Associated companies and representatives throughout the world.

Library of Congress Cataloging-in-Publication Data

Bruce, Linda, 1953-
    Household technology / by Linda Bruce and Ian Bruce.
        p. cm. -- (How does it work?)
    ISBN-13: 978-1-58340-797-4 (lg. print : hc : alk. Paper)
    1. Household electronics—Juvenile literature. I. Bruce, Ian. II. Title. III. Series.

TX298.B79 2006
643'.6—dc22

                                                                2005046772

Edited by Anna Fern
Text and cover design by Modern Art Production Group
Illustrations by Andrew Louey
Photo research by Legend Images

Printed in USA

Acknowledgments

The author and publishers are grateful to the following for permission to reproduce copyright material:

Cover photo: Toaster, courtesy of Rob Cruse Photography.

Australian Picture Library, p. 8; Corbis, p. 26; Rob Cruse Photography, pp. 1, 14, 16, 18; Istockphoto.com, pp. 9, 10, 11; Dale Mann Retrospect, p. 21; Photolibrary.com, pp. 5, 22, 24; Photos.com, p. 12; Productbank, pp. 15, 19, 20, 28, 30; Science Photo Library, p. 4, /Sheila Terry, p. 6, /Francoise Saulze, p. 17, /Gusto, p. 29.

While every care has been taken to trace and acknowledge copyright, the publisher tenders their apologies for any accidental infringement where copyright has proved untraceable. Where the attempt has been unsuccessful, the publisher welcomes information that would redress the situation.

Contents

Glossary words

When a word is printed in **bold**, you can look up its meaning in the Glossary on page 31.

What is technology?

Technology helps us to do things. Technology is also about how things work. Since ancient times, people have been interested in how things work, and how they can improve technology to meet their needs. They use their experience, knowledge, and ideas to invent new ways of doing things.

The *How Does It Work?* series features the design and technology of machines that are part of our daily lives. This includes:

- the purpose of the technology and its design
- where it is used
- how it is used
- materials it is made from
- how it works
- future developments

Technology has changed the way we live in many ways. It will keep on bringing change, as people constantly invent new ways of doing things using new materials.

Household technology keeps changing and developing.

4

Household technology

Household technology helps us to live more comfortably in our homes and to carry out daily household tasks.

New technology has changed the way we cook, keep food, wash, and clean. Lighting has changed from candles and oil lamps to lights powered by gas and electricity. Cooking has changed from wood stoves, to gas and electric stoves, to microwave ovens. Instead of boiling water in outside coppers on the wood stove, gas and electric hot water systems have been invented. To keep food cool, safes and ice-chests have been invented, and then refrigerators that ran on kerosene, gas, and electricity.

Many of these inventions greatly decreased the amount of time it takes to perform household tasks, creating time for us to spend on other activities.

This book takes an inside look at different kinds of household technology. It also previews some amazing new inventions in household technology that you might use in the future.

Technology helps to make many household chores much easier.

Circuits and switches

A **circuit** is a loop along which electricity flows. The flow of electricity, called a current, can only travel along a wire if there are no gaps. A switch is used to open or close a gap in the wire so that the electricity can be turned off or on.

Where used?

In houses, the circuit wires form a loop, running from the fuse box, through the walls and ceilings, and back again. Inside the house, outlets with switches make it possible for electrical appliances to be plugged into circuits.

How used?

People use circuits and switches every time they switch on electrical appliances, such as irons, toasters, and lights.

Materials

Circuits are made from metal wire covered with plastic **insulation**. Switches have metal parts for electricity to flow along and plastic covers to protect the person touching the switch from **electric shocks**. Switches are made in different colored plastics to match other colors in the room.

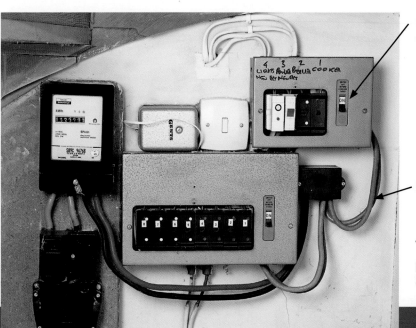

main power switch
outside the house

insulated wires

The fuse box supplies power to all the circuits inside a house.

How do circuits and switches work?

Electricity flows from the main switch outside the house along a circuit inside the house. When a light switch is turned on, electricity flows along the circuit to the lightbulb.

? Danger!

- Never push anything other than an electric plug into an outlet.
- When not using electrical appliances, switch them off at the outlet and unplug them.
- If you touch a switch when you have wet hands you may get a bad electric shock.

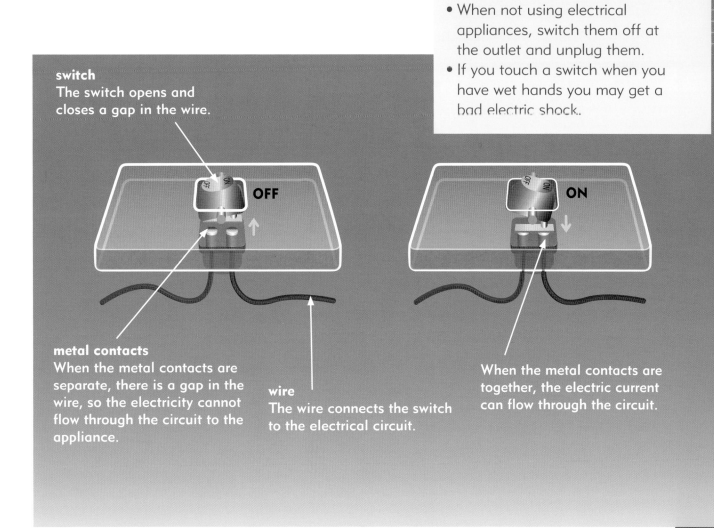

switch
The switch opens and closes a gap in the wire.

OFF

ON

metal contacts
When the metal contacts are separate, there is a gap in the wire, so the electricity cannot flow through the circuit to the appliance.

wire
The wire connects the switch to the electrical circuit.

When the metal contacts are together, the electric current can flow through the circuit.

What's next?

In the future, circuits will automatically check the condition of wires and will sound a beep to alert householders of dangerous faults in circuit wiring.

Remote controls

A remote control is used to control electrical appliances, such as televisions, video recorders, and CD players. Remote controls can turn the appliance on and off, change channels, and adjust volume without the person having to move from their seat.

Where used?

Remote controls are used wherever appliances are operated. They are also used to unlock car doors and open garage doors.

How used?

The remote control is held in one hand. It is pointed at the sensor in the television or other appliance, and the appropriate button pressed. Remote controls are powered by batteries.

Materials

The outer case and buttons of the remote control are made of plastic. The **circuitry** inside is mainly metal. The batteries contain chemicals to make electricity to power the remote control.

Remote controls make it possible for people to operate devices from a distance.

How do remote controls work?

When the buttons are pushed, the remote control sends a beam of **infrared light** pulses to a sensor in the television. Each button on the remote control sends a different pattern of pulses. The sensor detects the pattern and changes it to a command corresponding to the button being pressed.

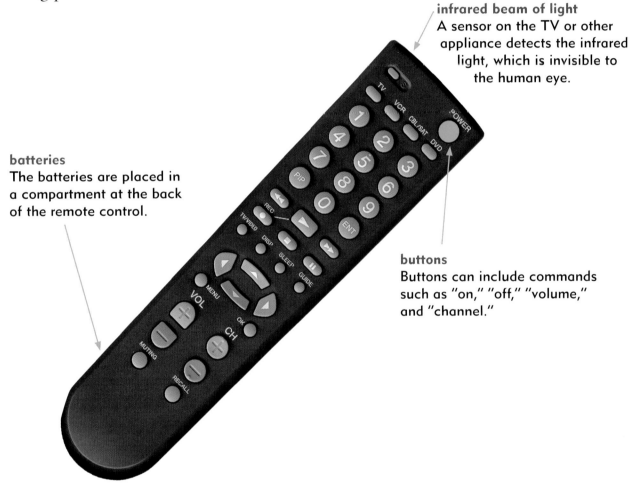

infrared beam of light
A sensor on the TV or other appliance detects the infrared light, which is invisible to the human eye.

batteries
The batteries are placed in a compartment at the back of the remote control.

buttons
Buttons can include commands such as "on," "off," "volume," and "channel."

What's next?

In the future, appliances will be able to be controlled by a person's thoughts. A sensor worn on the person's head will change their brain waves into an infrared signal, which can switch appliances, such as televisions and lights, on and off.

Lightbulbs

A lightbulb changes the energy from electricity into heat, which gives off a bright light that we can see by.

Where used?

Lightbulbs can be used in lamps plugged into an outlet, or in light fittings that are wired into the electrical circuit on house ceilings and walls.

How used?

When the user turns on a switch, electricity flows from the electricity circuit in the wall and along wires into the lightbulb, which turns the light on. Switching the electricity off at the light switch breaks the electrical circuit and the light turns off.

Materials

The lightbulb is made from glass to let light shine through. The electrical wires are made from metal, which conducts electricity easily. The part of the lightbulb that gives off light is made from a metal called tungsten.

Lightbulbs are called "incandescent," which means "glowing brightly."

How do lightbulbs work?

Most lightbulbs contain a thin, coiled wire, called a filament. When the filament heats up, it glows very brightly. The wire in some filaments is tightly coiled so that there is more wire in the filament. The more wire there is to heat up, the more light the lightbulb gives off.

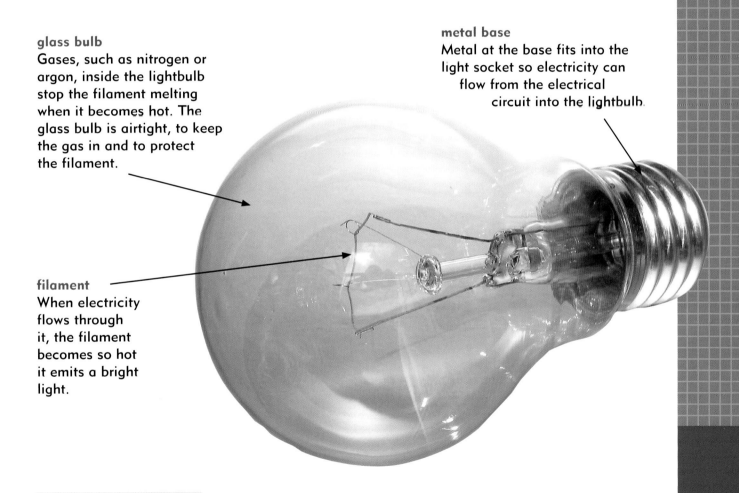

glass bulb
Gases, such as nitrogen or argon, inside the lightbulb stop the filament melting when it becomes hot. The glass bulb is airtight, to keep the gas in and to protect the filament.

metal base
Metal at the base fits into the light socket so electricity can flow from the electrical circuit into the lightbulb.

filament
When electricity flows through it, the filament becomes so hot it emits a bright light.

What's next?

In the future, lightbulbs will produce more light and less heat, and will use less electricity. Tungsten wire may be replaced by tungsten crystals, which reflect light without losing energy in the form of heat. Many lightbulbs may be replaced with light-emitting diodes (LEDs), which have no filament to burn out, and so last longer.

Flashlights and batteries

A flashlight is an electric light which can be carried. Flashlights consist of a portable power source, such as a battery, connected to a lightbulb.

Where used?

Flashlights are used when camping, walking in the dark, or looking into dark places.

How used?

Flashlights are carried in one hand. A switch on the side of the flashlight turns the light on. The beam of light can then be pointed in any direction.

Materials

The flashlight case is made from plastic, which does not break when dropped. To conduct electricity, battery cases and flashlight wires are made from metal. The lightbulb and its protective cover are made from glass so light can shine through.

How do flashlights work?

When the switch is turned on, it completes the circuit between the batteries and the lightbulb. The reflector behind the lightbulb directs the light forward. When the switch is turned off, the circuit is broken and electricity does not flow anywhere.

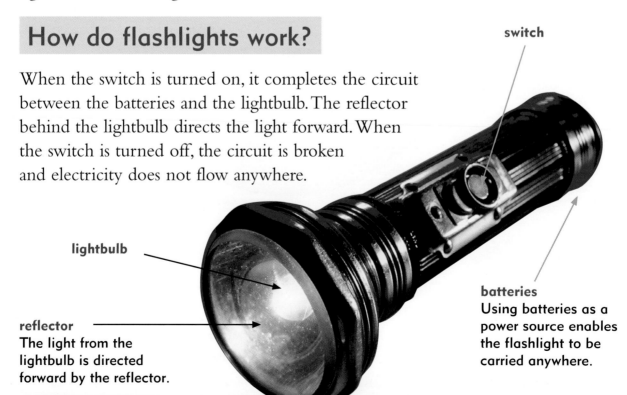

switch

lightbulb

reflector
The light from the lightbulb is directed forward by the reflector.

batteries
Using batteries as a power source enables the flashlight to be carried anywhere.

How do batteries work?

Batteries provide power by changing **chemical energy** into electrical energy. When one end of a wire is connected to the positive **electrode** and the other end of the wire to the negative electrode, a chemical reaction starts inside the battery. Electricity made by this reaction flows out of the negative end of the battery, through the wires, and into the flashlight or other appliance.

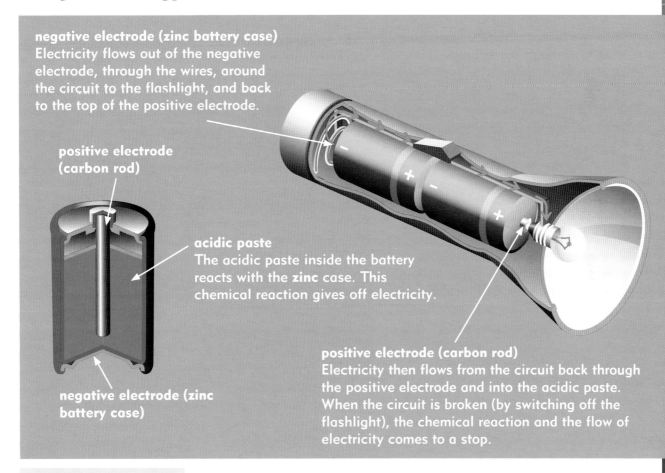

negative electrode (zinc battery case)
Electricity flows out of the negative electrode, through the wires, around the circuit to the flashlight, and back to the top of the positive electrode.

positive electrode (carbon rod)

acidic paste
The acidic paste inside the battery reacts with the **zinc** case. This chemical reaction gives off electricity.

negative electrode (zinc battery case)

positive electrode (carbon rod)
Electricity then flows from the circuit back through the positive electrode and into the acidic paste. When the circuit is broken (by switching off the flashlight), the chemical reaction and the flow of electricity comes to a stop.

What's next?

In the future, there may be mud batteries, which harness the energy given off by bacteria as they break down matter in mud.

Batteries may be replaced by tiny ceramic **generators** called micro-engines. These may generate 300 times more energy than an ordinary battery, but they may be less than one-tenth of an inch wide.

Electric jugs

An electric jug is used to boil water to make drinks, such as hot chocolate, tea, and coffee.

Where used?

Electric jugs usually sit on a kitchen counter close to an outlet.

How used?

Enough water is poured into the electric jug to cover the heating **element**. The lid is closed, the electric cord plugged into an outlet, and the switches on the outlet and jug are turned on. When the water has boiled, a safety switch automatically turns the jug off.

Materials

Jugs are made from metal or plastic, which are strong and lightweight. Materials are chosen so the jug does not burn the counter and the handle stays cool. The heating element inside the jug and the electric wires are made from metal.

Electric jugs heat water quickly and are easy to use.

How do electric jugs work?

When the jug is switched on, electricity flows out of the outlet on the wall, along the cord into the jug, and through an element inside the jug. The element becomes hot and heats the water surrounding it. The heated water rises and the cooler water sinks. Most jugs hold between two and six cups of water.

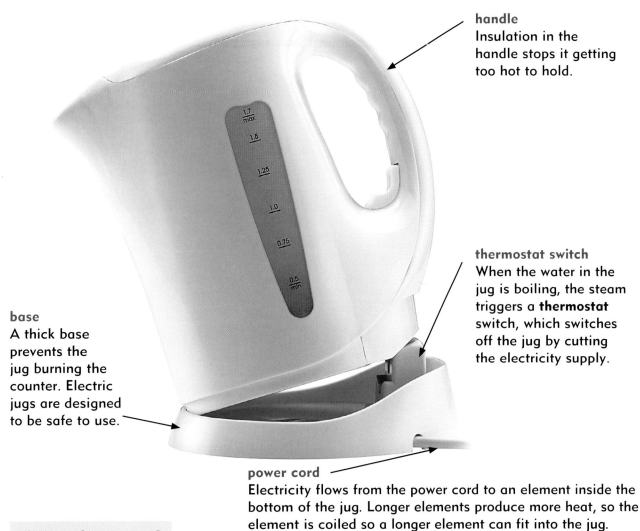

handle
Insulation in the handle stops it getting too hot to hold.

thermostat switch
When the water in the jug is boiling, the steam triggers a **thermostat** switch, which switches off the jug by cutting the electricity supply.

base
A thick base prevents the jug burning the counter. Electric jugs are designed to be safe to use.

power cord
Electricity flows from the power cord to an element inside the bottom of the jug. Longer elements produce more heat, so the element is coiled so a longer element can fit into the jug.

What's next?

In the future, jugs may use different ways of heating water, such as **microwaves**, which would use less energy. They may also be able to be switched on and off by the sound of a person's voice.

Electric toothbrushes

An electric toothbrush is a brush with revolving bristles powered by an electric motor. Electric toothbrushes clean teeth more effectively than brushing by hand.

Where used?

An electric toothbrush is used in the bathroom. It is kept near an outlet so the battery inside the toothbrush can be charged.

How used?

The electric toothbrush is held in one hand, switched on, and the bristles are pressed against the teeth. The bristles turn, brushing plaque and food off teeth and gums.

Materials

The brush handle and case are made from plastics that do not conduct electricity. The electric motor inside the handle is made from metal. The bristles are made of varying lengths of plastic.

An electric toothbrush makes it easier to remove plaque from every tooth.

How do electric toothbrushes work?

An electric toothbrush combines a rechargeable battery, an electric motor, gears, a switch, a simple lock to keep the toothbrush head on, and a plastic head with bristles.

To recharge the batteries in the toothbrush, the toothbrush rests on the base. The base contains one part of a coil around a metal bar, called a **transformer**. The handle of the toothbrush contains a second coil. When the base and toothbrush are fitted together, the electricity can recharge the battery inside the toothbrush handle.

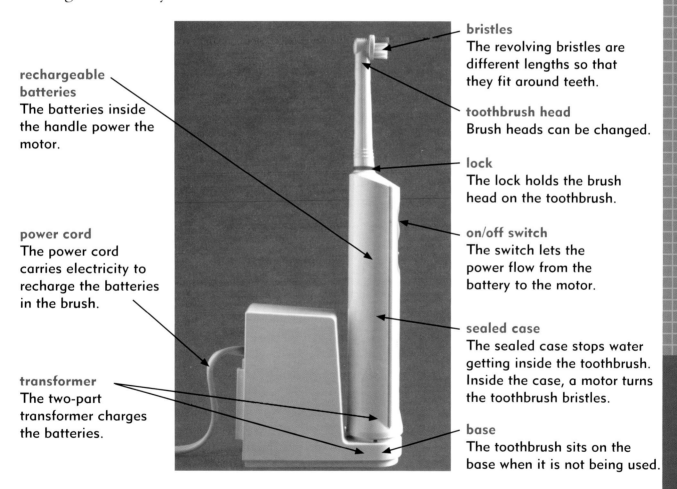

rechargeable batteries
The batteries inside the handle power the motor.

power cord
The power cord carries electricity to recharge the batteries in the brush.

transformer
The two-part transformer charges the batteries.

bristles
The revolving bristles are different lengths so that they fit around teeth.

toothbrush head
Brush heads can be changed.

lock
The lock holds the brush head on the toothbrush.

on/off switch
The switch lets the power flow from the battery to the motor.

sealed case
The sealed case stops water getting inside the toothbrush. Inside the case, a motor turns the toothbrush bristles.

base
The toothbrush sits on the base when it is not being used.

What's next?

In the future, electric toothbrushes may use a magnet to pull plaque off teeth and onto the bristles.

Toasters

A toaster is an electrical appliance that uses heated wires to toast bread.

Where used?

A toaster often sits on a kitchen counter near an outlet.

How used?

The user places a piece of bread into a slot in the toaster. The slot contains a metal holder. A lever at the end of the toaster is pushed to lower the bread into the toaster.

Materials

The outside of the toaster is made from metal or heat-resistant plastic. Inside the toaster, on each side of the slot, are sheets of nichrome wire coiled across a metal sheet. Nichrome wire is an **alloy** of nickel and chromium, which becomes very hot when electricity flows through it. The toaster handle is made from plastic that does not become hot or melt easily.

Toasters change electricity into heat, which toasts the bread.

How do electric toasters work?

When the toaster is turned on, electricity flows through wires on each side of the toast slot. The wires become hot and the heat that is given off cooks the toast. A timer determines cooking time.

Most toasters use an **electromagnet** to hold the toast rack down. An electromagnet works by having a **magnet** on one side and a piece of material that the magnet strongly attracts, such as iron or steel, on the other side. When the electricity is switched on, it activates the magnet, which keeps the toast holder down, and also switches on the toaster. When the electricity is switched off, the electromagnet switches off and the toast pops up.

coils
Inside the toaster, coils give off heat, which cooks the toast.

plastic handle

toast rack
An electromagnet holds the toast rack down.

toast rack lever
The lever is pushed to lower the bread into the toaster.

timer
The timer triggers a switch, which turns the toaster off. The timer can be adjusted to cook the perfect piece of toast.

What's next?

In the future, there may be voice-activated toasters, which will cook toast on command. There may also be mini-ovens with timers that can be activated by a signal sent over the Internet to cook toast at a specified time.

Sandwich toasters

A sandwich toaster is an electrical appliance that toasts sandwiches and seals the edges to hold in melted or runny fillings.

Where used?

Sandwich toasters are used on a counter in the kitchen, near an outlet.

How used?

The sandwich toaster is plugged in and switched on to heat. The lid is opened and one slice of buttered bread is placed spread-side down on the plate. Filling is placed on this bread. Another slice of buttered bread is placed on top with the spread-side facing up. The lid is closed and fastened. When the sandwich is toasted, a non-metal spoon or spatula is used to remove it without scratching the hotplates.

Materials

Sandwich toasters are mainly made from metal. A coating material, such as teflon, stops food sticking to the hotplates. Plastic indicator lights glow red when power to the sandwich toaster is switched on. The handle is made from heat-resistant plastic, which stays cool to touch.

Sandwich toasters seal the edges of the bread so that the hot filling stays inside the sandwich.

How do sandwich toasters work?

A sandwich toaster has two molded non-stick hotplates with a hinge between them. When the sandwich is placed inside, the plates cut and seal it into two easy-to-handle triangular sandwiches.

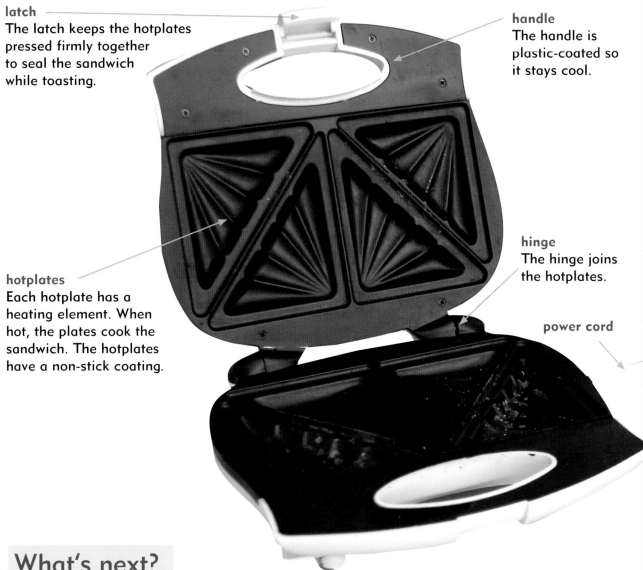

latch
The latch keeps the hotplates pressed firmly together to seal the sandwich while toasting.

handle
The handle is plastic-coated so it stays cool.

hinge
The hinge joins the hotplates.

power cord

hotplates
Each hotplate has a heating element. When hot, the plates cook the sandwich. The hotplates have a non-stick coating.

What's next?

In the future, sandwich toasters may have ceramic hotplates. Ceramic is made from clay, just like china plates, and the tiles on a space **shuttle**. Ceramic hotplates are more efficient at holding uniform heat and keep the sandwich filling moist.

Refrigerators

A refrigerator is an insulated container in which food is cooled and stored. Refrigeration helps the food to last longer because low temperatures slow down the growth of bacteria.

Where used?

A refrigerator usually stands in the kitchen near an outlet and counter where food is prepared.

How used?

The contents of refrigerators are easy to access by a door on the front. Food is placed on racks within the refrigerator body, or in the freezer to be frozen. A control or dial inside the refrigerator allows the temperature to be adjusted.

Materials

Refrigerators are mostly made from strong metal that lasts a long time. Many shelves and containers inside are made from light, easy-to-clean plastic. Sometimes, ammonia gas is used to keep the refrigerator cold.

Opening a refrigerator door too often means that the refrigerator must work harder and use more energy to stay cool.

How do refrigerators work?

A refrigerator works by moving heat from inside to outside. This makes the inside cold. The refrigerator has a loop of pipe that runs inside and outside of it. The motor pumps a gas, called a refrigerant, through the pipe.

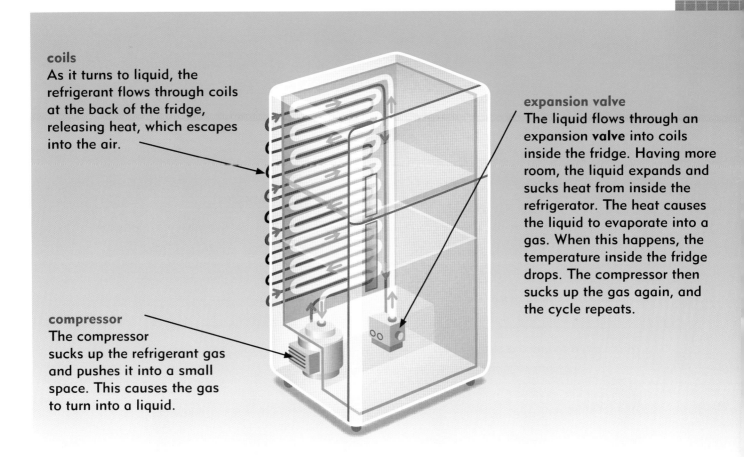

coils
As it turns to liquid, the refrigerant flows through coils at the back of the fridge, releasing heat, which escapes into the air.

expansion valve
The liquid flows through an expansion **valve** into coils inside the fridge. Having more room, the liquid expands and sucks heat from inside the refrigerator. The heat causes the liquid to evaporate into a gas. When this happens, the temperature inside the fridge drops. The compressor then sucks up the gas again, and the cycle repeats.

compressor
The compressor sucks up the refrigerant gas and pushes it into a small space. This causes the gas to turn into a liquid.

What's next?

In the future, you may be able to log on to your refrigerator over the Internet to check items, such as margarine or eggs, that are in low supply. The refrigerator will do this by weighing food on different shelves and making a list. This may allow people at work to find out which foods they need to buy before they return home.

Microwave ovens

A microwave oven uses microwaves to cook food more quickly than traditional ovens do.

Where used?

A microwave oven sits on the kitchen counter near an outlet.

How used?

The door of the microwave oven is opened and the food to be heated is placed on a turntable inside. The oven door is closed, and control buttons are pressed to choose heat intensity and cooking time.

Materials

Microwave ovens are made mainly from metal. Glass in the door provides a view of food cooking. A metal mesh inside the door stops microwaves from traveling through the glass. Control buttons are plastic. The plate inside the oven is glass, which does not easily crack.

Microwave ovens are simple to use.

How do microwave ovens work?

A microwave oven uses invisible waves of energy, called microwaves, to cook food. Microwaves vibrate water **molecules** within food, heating them. This heat passes through the food, cooking it from within.

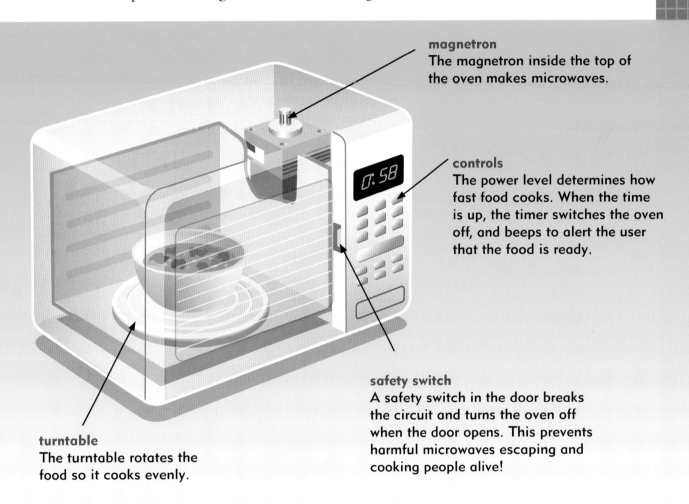

magnetron
The magnetron inside the top of the oven makes microwaves.

controls
The power level determines how fast food cooks. When the time is up, the timer switches the oven off, and beeps to alert the user that the food is ready.

safety switch
A safety switch in the door breaks the circuit and turns the oven off when the door opens. This prevents harmful microwaves escaping and cooking people alive!

turntable
The turntable rotates the food so it cooks evenly.

What's next?

In the future, microwave ovens may be able to be turned on remotely, by using a signal sent via the Internet. There may also be machines that look like microwave ovens, but which are used to instantly freeze food.

Landline telephones

A landline telephone enables people to talk to each other over long distances, and connect to the Internet. Modern telephone lines can also carry cable TV and computer games.

Where used?

Telephones are often placed on office desks, or on a counter in the kitchen, lounge, or bedroom. All landline telephones need a connection to a telephone line. Cordless telephones also need electricity to charge the batteries within their handsets.

How used?

Users hold the handset and press the telephone number of the person to be contacted on the keypad. The signal travels to its destination and rings the telephone there. The person receiving the call picks up the handset, speaks into it, and listens.

Materials

Telephones are mainly made from light, cheap, durable plastic. Smaller internal parts are made from metal, which easily conducts electrical signals. Telephone calls travel by radio and along **cables** made from metal or glass.

handset

stretchable cord

keypad

People use telephones to talk with each other.

How do telephones work?

A telephone changes the caller's voice into electrical signals. When the electrical signal reaches the earpiece of the receiver's telephone, the signal is changed back into sound.

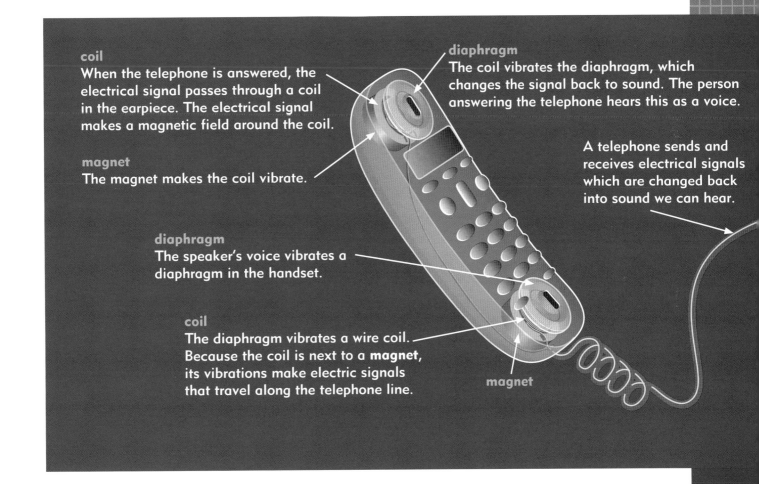

coil
When the telephone is answered, the electrical signal passes through a coil in the earpiece. The electrical signal makes a magnetic field around the coil.

magnet
The magnet makes the coil vibrate.

diaphragm
The speaker's voice vibrates a diaphragm in the handset.

coil
The diaphragm vibrates a wire coil. Because the coil is next to a **magnet**, its vibrations make electric signals that travel along the telephone line.

diaphragm
The coil vibrates the diaphragm, which changes the signal back to sound. The person answering the telephone hears this as a voice.

A telephone sends and receives electrical signals which are changed back into sound we can hear.

magnet

What's next?

In the future, landline telephones used at home will use the same line as cable television and the Internet. People will be able to watch television while waiting for a call, as well as being able to send and receive emails and text messages.

Vacuum cleaners

A **vacuum** cleaner is an electrical appliance that is used to suck dirt and dust from floors and carpets.

Where used?

Vacuum cleaners are usually used inside buildings where there is a power connection.

How used?

The person using the vacuum cleaner plugs it into an outlet and turns the power on. The electricity flows along the power cord to the cleaner. The operator uses their hand or foot to press a button on the vacuum cleaner to start the machine. The bag inside the vacuum cleaner that collects the dust needs to be emptied when it is full.

Materials

The body of a cleaner is often made from metal alloy and plastic. The engine and fan are made from metal, and the hoses and nozzles are often plastic.

Vacuum cleaners suck dirt from floors and carpets.

How do vacuum cleaners work?

Vacuum cleaners work by sucking dirt into a bag or chamber. The electric motor spins a fan, which blows air out the back of the cleaner. This causes air to be sucked in through the hose at the front of the machine.

bag
The filter blocks the dirt and dust, which collects in the bag. The air passes through the filter to the fan and out the back of the vacuum cleaner.

fan
When the fan spins, it blows air out the back of the cleaner. This creates a vacuum, causing air to be sucked in through the hose at the front of the cleaner.

electric motor
The electric motor spins a fan.

hose

tube

filter

cleaning head
The cleaning head rubs and loosens dirt and dust, which is then sucked up through the hose.

What's next?

In the future, we may use robot vacuum cleaners, which can be started remotely or set to start vacuuming at a specified time. They will recognize items that should not be vacuumed, such as socks and cats.

29

How well does it work?

In this book you have read about and looked at the designs of many different technologies. As well as understanding how technology works, we also need to think about how well it works in relation to other needs, such as aesthetic, environmental, and social needs. We can judge how well the idea, product, or process works by considering questions, such as:

Manufacture	• Is the manufacture of the technology efficient in its use of energy and resources?
Usability	• Does the technology do the job it is designed to do? • Is it safe to use? • Is it easy to use?
Social impact	• Does it have any negative effects on people?
Environmental impact	• Does using the technology have any environmental effects? • Does it create noise, cause pollution, or create any waste products?
Aesthetics	• Does the design fit into its surroundings and look attractive?

Thinking about these sorts of questions can help people to invent improved ways of doing things.

Internet refrigerators like this one will soon be found in many modern kitchens.

Glossary

alloy a mixture of metals

cable thick bundle of electrical wires that are bound together and insulated

chemical energy the energy given off by chemical reactions

circuit a path between two or more points along which an electrical current or signal can be carried

circuitry a system of electrical circuits

electric shocks the effects of an electric current going through a body

electrode conductor through which electricity flows

electromagnet a magnet that needs electricity to activate it

element the wire that becomes hot in a heating device

generators machines used to make electricity

infrared light a wavelength of electromagnetic radiation that is similar to the wavelength of red light, but which is invisible to the human eye

insulation material that blocks electricity or heat from flowing through it

magnet metal that can pull iron or steel objects toward it and hold or move them

microwaves invisible electromagnetic radiation

molecules the smallest particles of a substance

shuttle a spacecraft launched by rocket, that returns to Earth to be launched again

thermostat a device that controls temperature by switching off when too hot, or on when too cold

transformer a device that increases or decreases the strength of an electric current

vacuum space with very little or no air in it

valve a moveable part that opens, closes or partially blocks a pipe to control the flow of liquid, gas, or air

zinc a bluish-white metal

Index